YEAR L[...]
MINIST[...]

CW00531667

The publisher of this [...]
You'll get quick ideas [...]
year. Discussion sta[...]
Meetings. Bible stud[...]
more—mail this car[...]

❑ **YES!** Start my no-risk subscription to GROUP
Magazine. Bill me at the special introductory 1-year rate of
$21.95 ($4 off!). I understand that this subscription is completely guaranteed.

Name _____

Address _____

City _____

State _____ ZIP _____

P114G

GUARANTEE: If you're ever disappointed in GROUP, just
tell us. We'll refund you for all unmailed issues and cancel
your subscription. No questions asked.

QUICK HELP TO REACH
JUNIOR HIGHERS!

JR. HIGH MINISTRY—from the publisher of this
book—brings you complete meetings. Trends. Help
for parents. Quick ideas. And special feature arti-
cles to help you reach this not-quite-teenage group
of kids. Try a no-risk subscription by mailing this
card today.

❑ **YES!** Start my no-risk, 1-year subscription to
JR. HIGH MINISTRY Magazine for $19.95. I
understand that this subscription is completely
guaranteed.

Name _____

Address _____

City _____

State _____ ZIP _____

P114J

GUARANTEE: If JR. HIGH MINISTRY ever disappoints you,
just tell us. We'll refund you for all unmailed issues and cancel your subscription. No questions asked.

BUSINESS REPLY MAIL
FIRST CLASS MAIL   PERMIT NO. 25   MT. MORRIS, IL

POSTAGE WILL BE PAID BY ADDRESSEE

Group®
Box 202
Mt. Morris, IL 61054-9816

||||||||||||||||||||||||||||||||||||||||||||||||||||||

BUSINESS REPLY MAIL
FIRST CLASS MAIL   PERMIT NO. 26   MT. MORRIS, IL

POSTAGE WILL BE PAID BY ADDRESSEE

**JR.HIGH
MINISTRY**
Box 407
Mt. Morris, IL 61054-9814

||||||||||||||||||||||||||||||||||||||||||||||||||||||

Devotions for Youth Groups on the Go

By
Dan and Cindy Hansen

Loveland, Colorado

Dedication

● To our three sons—Stevie, Tommy and Matty—
three wonderful boys who are
always
"on the go"

● To Dan's Grandma Lien, who recently died—
a dedicated Sunday school teacher and church woman
"on the go"
for 97 years

Devotions for Youth Groups on the Go

Copyright © 1992 Dan and Cindy Hansen

First Printing

Credits
Edited by Michael Warden
Cover designed by DeWain Stoll
Interior designed by Dori Walker
Interior illustrations by Rand Kruback

Scriptures quoted from The Youth Bible, New Century Version, copyright ©1991 by Word Publishing, Dallas, Texas 75039. Used by permission.

ISBN 1-55945-075-4

Printed in the United States of America

Contents

Devotions to Go

Introduction

Devotions for Youth Groups On the Go contains 52 fun, interesting and faith-building devotions to take with you and your group wherever you go—from amusement parks and ball games to rafting trips and kite-flying contests.

You also get three unique devotions for the time between "here" and "there" or when those inevitable mishaps come your way. The devotions are called "On the Way to an Activity," "When the Van Breaks Down" and "When Bad Weather Cancels an Event." (See pages 103 to 107.)

Devotion Details

These "on the go" devotions are easy to prepare—few props are needed. All the questions and activities revolve around the actual event—the world becomes your playground and classroom all in one!

Each devotion suggests a time and place to gather for Bible study and prayer during your outing. If having the devotion at the location won't work for you, just do it when you get back to your church. The time and place are up to you.

Each devotion is divided into three parts.

● **Theme:** This is the devotion's topic and focus. Themes cover a variety of teenagers' needs and concerns.

● **Scripture to Go:** Each devotion is based on a scripture that supports the theme and teaches kids God's love.

● **Devotion to Go:** Kids use their senses to "experience" and gain a deeper understanding of the topic and how it applies to their lives. Each devotion includes scripture reading, activities, discussion questions and prayer.

May God bless you and your youth group as you continue to help kids grow. Just stick with Jesus in all you do—you'll go places!

1 Amusement Park

Theme:
Body of Christ

> **Scripture to Go: 1 Corinthians 12:19-21, 25b-27**
> Truly God put all the parts, each one of them, in the body as he want-
> ed them. So then there are many parts, but only one body. The eye
> cannot say to the hand, "I don't need you!" And the head cannot say
> to the foot, "I don't need you!" ... God wanted the different parts to
> care the same for each other. If one part of the body suffers, all the
> other parts suffer with it. Or if one part of our body is honored, all the
> other parts share its honor. Together you are the body of Christ, and
> each one of you is a part of that body.

Devotion to Go

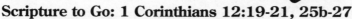

Gather at a refreshment stand
halfway through your amuse-
ment-park outing. Allow time for
kids to buy snacks. Then gather
for devotions.

Ask each person to describe
his or her favorite ride so far.
Form pairs by having kids get
with a person who described a
similar favorite ride. Have pairs

each make a human sculpture
that represents their favorite
ride. For example, a sculpture for
a roller coaster could be kids
"gripping" the safety bar—mouth
and eyes wide open.

Note the variety of favorites.
Then ask: **How did you feel
riding your favorite ride? Why
is it your favorite? What did
you notice about the variety of
sculptures and the variety of**

opinions? How are the differences in our sculptures like the differences in the body of Christ?

Ask a person sitting on your right to read aloud 1 Corinthians 12:19-21, 25b-27. Ask: **What does the scripture tell us about each other? What does this mean, "There are many parts, but only one body"?** Say: **All of us came as one group to the amusement park, but we each like different rides. We're all different—with unique likes, dislikes and abilities—but we are one body of Christ. The scripture says, "God wanted the different parts to care the same for each other."**

Go around the group and let each person describe a gift or ability they see in someone in the group, such as the ability to make people feel welcome, the ability to have fun in any situation, or the ability to sing or play a musical instrument. Ask: **How can that gift be used in our church? at school? at home?**

Close with a time of "honoring" each person. Start with the person who read the scripture. Let kids each say one way this person is a powerful part of Christ's body. Let each person have a chance at being "honored."

Pray: **God, help us honor others, because we'll be honored at the same time. Thanks for making each one of us as you wanted. Thanks for helping us work together as Christ's body. In Jesus' name, amen.**

Backpacking

Theme: Environment

Scripture to Go: Psalm 65:9-13
You take care of the land and water it; you make it very fertile. The rivers of God are full of water. Grain grows because you make it grow. You send rain to the plowed fields; you fill the rows with water. You soften the ground with rain, and then you bless it with crops. You give the year a good harvest, and you load the wagons with many crops. The desert is covered with grass and the hills with happiness. The pastures are full of flocks, and the valleys are covered with grain. Everything shouts and sings for joy.

Devotion to Go

Regardless of where you've backpacked—the foothills, a woods, a national park—enjoy your surroundings by going on a "nature treasure hunt."

Give group members a moment to find a nature treasure, such as a flower, nest or tree. One at a time, have kids lead the others to their treasures. This way kids can enjoy nature as it is—not disturbing nests or picking wildflowers.

As kids show their treasures, ask: **How did it feel to find this treasure? What does this nature treasure tell us about God?**

Have the last person who showed a nature treasure read aloud Psalm 65:9-13, pausing briefly after each sentence. Ask:

What does this passage tell us about treasures in nature? How do you think God feels when people pollute the earth? What do you and your family do to protect the environment? How can we begin to care for the environment more effectively?

Close by letting backpackers "retell" the Psalm as a prayer by filling in the blanks of the following sentences according to what kids see around them:

● God, you take care of ...

● ... grows because you make it grow.

● You send rain to ...

● Our surroundings are covered with ...

● We shout and sing for joy because of ...

● Amen!

3 Ball Game

Theme: Forgiveness

Scripture to Go: Matthew 18:21-22
Then Peter came to Jesus and asked, "Lord, when my fellow believer sins against me, how many times must I forgive him? Should I forgive him as many as seven times?"

Jesus answered, "I tell you, you must forgive him more than seven times. You must forgive him even if he does wrong to you seventy-seven times."

Devotion to Go

Gather for a devotion after the game. Buy several bags of peanuts.

Tell kids they're going to talk about forgiving seventy-seven times. To do this, pass around the bags of peanuts, and have each person take seven. Tell them not to eat their peanuts until later.

Have kids work in pairs. For each of the first seven peanuts, have pairs discuss seven sins they have trouble forgiving others for, such as others talking behind their backs, saying they'll do somethings then not doing it, picking fights and stealing. Ask: **How do you feel when people sin against you this way? Why are these sins so hard to forgive?**

For each of the other seven peanuts, have pairs discuss seven sins that they have trouble forgiving themselves for, such as lying to parents, cheating on a test, procrastinating and gossiping. Ask: **How do you feel when you do these things? Why is it hard to forgive yourself?**

Ask someone who cheered the loudest in the game to read aloud Matthew 18:21-22. Say: **In baseball or softball, you get three strikes and then you're out.** Ask: **With God, how many strikes does he give us before we're out? What does this passage tell us about the number of times we need to forgive others? ourselves? How can forgiving others and ourselves help our self-esteem?**

Have pairs take turns "batting" the peanuts into each other's mouths. ("Fly balls" are easiest to catch!) Each time they catch and eat a peanut, have them say, "You're forgiven." Ask: **How is batting the peanut away like forgiving? How can we learn to forgive others and forgive ourselves—then bat the memory away and not bring it up again?**

Close by asking kids to silently think of someone they need to forgive. Then have them think of one thing they need to forgive themselves for. Pray: **God, thanks for your forgiveness. Thanks for not keeping score of our sins. Help us do the same with our family, our friends and ourselves. Amen.**

Enjoy the rest of the peanuts!

4 Basketball Game

Theme: Think before you speak

> **Scripture to Go: Proverbs 13:3; 15:1; 20:19**
> Those who are careful about what they say protect their lives, but whoever speaks without thinking will be ruined ... A gentle answer will calm a person's anger, but an unkind answer will cause more anger ... Gossips can't keep secrets, so avoid people who talk too much.

Devotion to Go

At halftime, buy snacks, then gather in a quiet hallway.

Say: **We've seen a lot of fouls during this game. Fouls happen when players go against the rules. Fouls may hurt others. Fouls in real life are the hurtful things we say and do to others.**

Have three people read the three verses from Proverbs. Ask: **How do we "foul" or hurt others by saying things without thinking? What are some unkind things you've heard people say? How do you feel about hearing things like that? What have you said that you now regret?**

Have kids tell about times when they intentionally or unintentionally hurt another person with words. Mark a "free throw line" a few feet from a trash can. Have kids crumple their empty snack containers or napkins to represent the hurt they caused, then take turns making foul shots—throwing the trash in the trash can. After they make their shots, have them pray silently, asking God for forgiveness.

As a group, list ways to avoid fouls, such as thinking before you speak, talking nicely, not gossiping, guarding your words like the basketball players guard their opponents. Find a pencil, and write the ideas on an extra snack napkin. Ask kids to keep their napkins as a reminder to avoid "fouling" others this week.

Before you head back to the basketball game, pray: **Help us, God, to always speak well of others in the kindest way. In Jesus' name, amen!**

5 Beach

Theme: Blessings

Scripture to Go: Genesis 22:17-18
"I will surely bless you and give you many descendants. They will be as many as the stars in the sky and the sand on the seashore, and they will capture the cities of their enemies. Through your descendants all the nations on the earth will be blessed, because you obeyed me."

Devotion to Go

Enjoy a fun time in the sun. Swim, soak up the heat, have a picnic. When you're ready for a break, gather in a circle for a devotion.

Have kids each scoop up some sand in their hands. Ask them to let the sand slowly trickle out of their fingers and listen while you read aloud Genesis 22:17-18. Say: **Because Abraham obeyed God, God told him his de-** scendants would be as numerous as the sand on the shore. Ask: **How did hearing this passage make you feel as you sifted sand through your fingers? How did Abraham obey God? What blessings does God give us when we obey? What examples can you think of when disobedience has gotten people in trouble?**

Tell kids to gather exactly five grains of sand in their hands, then come up with five blessings in their lives that each grain represents. Have kids each share their blessings. Then have them look down the beach in both directions. Ask: **How did you feel about your blessings when you were looking at the five grains of sand in your hand? How did you feel when you compared your five grains to all the sand you see on the beach around us? How is all the sand on the beach like God's blessing in our lives? How are we sometimes like people who stand on a beach and concentrate on only five grains of sand? What can we do to "take in" more of God's blessings in our lives?**

Pray: **Your blessings, God, are as numerous as the grains of sand on the seashore. Help us to see your blessings in our lives and use them to bless others. In Jesus' name, amen.**

Bike Hike

6

Theme:
God's guidance

Scripture to Go: Psalm 119:105-106
Your word is like a lamp for my feet and a light for my path. I will do what I have promised and obey your fair laws.

Devotion to Go

Familiarize yourself with your bike route. Locate a bumpy dirt road or rough path about halfway through your route that you can lead kids to for this devotion.

Gather kids prior to taking off on your bike hike. Read aloud Psalm 119:105-106. Ask: **How does this passage make you feel about God's guidance?** Say: **God will guide our path today on the bike hike, and all our days. Let's put on our bike helmets to symbolize God's love, protection and guidance.**

At a halfway point during your bike hike, lead kids off the main road to a bumpy dirt road or path. Stop and ask: **How do you feel wandering from the main road to this spot off the beaten path? How is this like what happens when we don't follow God's guidance? What are ways we can seek God's guidance in our lives?** Say: **God's Word guides our lives, and God's love surrounds us everywhere.** Ask: **What are some ways you believe God has been looking out for you—or guiding you—during** this bike hike? during your daily life? How does God's guidance in the past give us courage for the future?

When you return to your starting point, get off your bikes, do a few stretches and let kids cool down from the exercise. Say: **Let's join hands in a circle to symbolize our support for each other. Think of one person who's been a support for you today or in your everyday life. Go around the circle and name that person.**

Allow time for kids each to name someone. Close by praying: **God, thanks for surrounding us with people who love us and support us and guide us. Help us to show your love to others by supporting them with encouragement and listening ears. Thanks for the signs of your love and guidance we saw on our bike hike. You are truly our great and loving God. In Jesus' name, amen.**

7 Boating

Theme: Faith

Scripture to Go: Matthew 14:25-32

Between three and six o'clock in the morning, Jesus came to them, walking on the water. When his followers saw him walking on the water, they were afraid. They said, "It's a ghost!" and cried out in fear.

But Jesus quickly spoke to them, "Have courage! It is I. Do not be afraid."

Peter said, "Lord, if it is really you, then command me to come to you on the water."

Jesus said, "Come."

And Peter left the boat and walked on the water to Jesus. But when Peter saw the wind and the waves, he became afraid and began to sink. He shouted, "Lord, save me!"

Immediately Jesus reached out his hand and caught Peter. Jesus said, "Your faith is small. Why did you doubt?"

After they got into the boat, the wind became calm. Then those who were in the boat worshiped Jesus and said, "Truly you are the Son of God!"

Devotion to Go

Before you get in your boats, gather around the shore and try this sink-or-float experiment. Have a small rock and a board close by.

Hold up the rock and ask:

How many of you believe this rock can float? Notice the disbelief. Have several kids test the rock to see if it will float. Then place the rock on the board and float it in the water. Ask: **How did it feel to try to float the rock? How did your attitude change when I floated the rock on the board? How is floating the rock on the board like living our lives by faith in Jesus? How does our faith keep us "afloat" through life's difficulties?** Say: **In our devotion in the boats, we'll talk about our faith. It keeps us afloat through difficulties in life.**

Once you're in the boat, ask one person to read aloud Matthew 14:25-32. Ask: **When have you, like Peter, started out with great intentions, but then began to "have your doubts"? How does our faith help us through doubtful times and scary storms in life?**

Ask kids to look around them for a symbol of their level of faith right now. One at a time, have kids each share their symbol. For example, "My faith is like the water—calm, comfortable," or "My faith is like this life jacket—it keeps me safe from drowning in my worries." Ask: **How can we strengthen our faith?** Have kids each tell a person sitting close to them one specific way they'll try to keep their faith strong and alive.

Close by having kids listen to the water lap at the boat, feel the wind on their faces, smell the fresh air. If you're close enough to the water, have them cup their hands in it and feel its coolness. Reread the passage, then pray: **God, give us courage and faith! Help us realize that you listen to us when we pray to you. Help us know you'll help us through all of life's storms. In Jesus' name, amen.**

8 Bonfire

Theme:
God's power

Scripture to Go: Hebrews 12:28-29
So let us be thankful, because we have a kingdom that cannot be shaken. We should worship God in a way that pleases him with respect and fear, because our God is like a fire that burns things up.

Devotion to Go

Gather around the fire. Sing songs such as, "Pass It On" or "Hear, Oh Israel."

Ask a person on your left to read aloud Hebrews 12:28-29. Ask kids each to find a piece of grass or a twig. Say: **Think of a situation or problem in your life that could use the touch of God's power. Your piece of grass or twig symbolizes this problem. Toss it in the fire and watch it burn. Ask: How did it feel to watch your twig or grass burn? How is that** like experiencing God's power in your life? How is the warmth of the fire like the warmth of God's presence?

Have kids turn around and feel the difference of the cool air, without the warmth of the fire. Ask: **How does the air feel facing away from the fire? How's the absence of God in your life like the cool night air? How can we work to keep God's presence and power active in our lives?**

Join hands in a circle around the fire. Guide kids in a silent prayer by saying: **Close your** eyes. Respond silently each time I pause. God, help us seek your powerful presence this week by worshiping you, praying with friends or some other way we name right now (*pause*). Thanks for your warm, firelike qualities. Thanks also for guiding us in our daily lives. Help us in these situations (*pause*). We love you. In Jesus' name, amen.

9 Bowling

Theme: Families

Scripture to Go: Luke 8:19-21
Jesus' mother and brothers came to see him, but there was such a crowd they could not get to him. Someone said to Jesus, "Your mother and your brothers are standing outside, wanting to see you."

Jesus answered them. "My mother and my brothers are those who listen to God's teaching and obey it."

Devotion to Go

Bowl a game or two to let kids warm up. Then gather for a devotion.

For this devotion, set up the pins as though you were going to play a fresh game. Tell kids they're going to have a gutter-ball contest. Have kids compete to see who can bowl the most creative or the most humorous "gutter ball." After everyone has bowled a gutter ball, vote on the most creative and the most fun

gutter balls. Ask: **How did you feel bowling only gutter balls? How does bowling gutter balls go against the purpose of the game? What is the goal in bowling?**

Ask kids to compare their experience with life in their families. Ask: **What's the "goal" in families? How is bowling gutter balls like the way we sometimes deal with our families? How have other family members bowled gutter balls in your life? How have you** bowled gutter balls in their lives? What are some specific ways we can avoid bowling gutter balls in our families?

Have the person who won the most creative award read aloud Luke 8:19-21. Ask: **What did Jesus mean in this passage? How was Jesus redefining "family" here? Do you believe the church can be a family to us? How? In what sense can our church family provide support? How can we avoid gutter balls in our church family?**

Ask a bowling lane employee for extra pencils and score sheets. Rip the sheets, so each person has one 10-frame strip.

On the first half of their strip, have kids each write five ideas for strengthening their immediate family—one idea per frame. Then, on the second half of their strip, have them write five ideas for strengthening their church family—one idea per frame.

Have kids pair off according to family size, and have them each tell their partner their idea. Have pairs each choose one idea from each category to start on this week.

Close by praying: **Our Father in heaven, thank you for the support of our church family. Help us strengthen our ties with each other and live as you would have us live. In Jesus' name, amen.**

10 Camping

Theme: Temptation

Scripture to Go: Matthew 4:1-11

Then the Spirit led Jesus into the desert to be tempted by the devil. Jesus ate nothing for forty days and nights. After this, he was very hungry. The devil came to Jesus to tempt him, saying, "If you are the Son of God, tell these rocks to become bread."

Jesus answered, "It is written in the Scriptures, 'A person does not live by eating only bread, but by everything God says.'"

Then the devil led Jesus to the holy city of Jerusalem and put him on a high place of the Temple. The devil said, "If you are the Son of God, jump down, because it is written in the Scriptures: 'He has put his angels in charge of you. They will catch you in their hands so that you will not hit your foot on a rock.'"

Jesus answered him, "It also says in the Scriptures, 'Do not test the Lord your God.'"

Then the devil led Jesus to the top of a very high mountain and showed him all the kingdoms of the world and all their splendor. The devil said, "If you will bow down and worship me, I will give you all these things."

Jesus said to the devil, "Go away from me, Satan! It is written in the Scriptures, 'You must worship the Lord your God and serve only him.'"

So the devil left Jesus, and angels came and took care of him.

Devotion to Go

Prior to supper, when the kids are hungry, gather for this devotion. Tell kids they're going to walk with Jesus through his temptations in the wilderness.

Lead your group to some big rocks. Ask everyone to sit down and get comfortable while you read about the devil trying to tempt Jesus to turn the rocks into bread (Matthew 4:3-4). Ask: **How do you feel right now before we eat? How do you think Jesus felt going 40 days and nights without food? What kinds of things besides food do you hunger for? How can those things keep you from God?**

Take everyone to a high place, such as a cliff or a large boulder. Read about the devil tempting Jesus to throw himself off and let the angels catch him (Matthew 4:5-7). Have kids stand on the edge of the cliff. Caution kids to not get *too* close to the edge. Ask: **How do you think Jesus felt when the devil tempted him to jump? When have you felt tempted to "take a leap" you knew you shouldn't? What did you do?**

Take group members to another high place where they can look at their entire surroundings. Read about the devil offering Jesus all he sees if he would just bow down and worship him (Matthew 4:8-10). Ask: **How do you think Jesus felt when the devil tempted him like this? If I told you, "I'll give you everything you see if you just bow down before me," would you be tempted? Why or why not? What material things are we tempted with today? What material things draw us away from God?**

Gather everyone back at the campsite. Give everyone a pre-supper snack such as an apple. Say: **Angels came and took care of Jesus just like they do for us when we turn away from temptation.**

Have kids each turn to a person sitting close to them and discuss: **Which of the three temptations pulls at you the most—satisfying your appetites, living recklessly, or desiring power and possessions? How can you let God help you deal with these temptations?**

Pray: **God, lead us not into temptation, but deliver us from evil. In Jesus' name, amen.**

11 Canoe Trip

Theme: Trust in God

Scripture to Go: Jeremiah 17:7-8
But the person who trusts in the Lord will be blessed. The Lord will show him that he can be trusted. He will be strong, like a tree planted near water that sends its roots by a stream. It is not afraid when the days are hot; its leaves are always green. It does not worry in a year when no rain comes; it always produces fruit.

Devotion to Go

Photocopy this devotion so each canoe-load of kids has one. If you're canoeing on a lake or pond, gather canoes in the middle to continue the devotion. If you're on a river, gather at a calm place on the shore. Point out the green vegetation along the banks of the river, stream or lake you're on.

Ask kids each to pick out the most beautiful tree they see along the shore. Have kids tell why they chose the tree they did. Ask: **What makes your tree so beautiful and strong? What keeps it healthy? How is your life like that tree?**

Ask kids to look at their trees as you read aloud Jeremiah 17: 7-8. Ask: **How is trusting God like planting a tree near the water? If you had to choose one of these trees to represent how close you are to** trusting God with your whole life, which tree would you choose?

After kids tell which trees they chose, ask: **Why do you find it hard to trust God in some areas of your life? How can we move toward trusting him more?**

Ask kids each to complete this sentence: "I will build my trust in God this week by..." For example, "I will build my trust in God this week by not worrying about my math test results," or "I will build my trust in God this week by bringing a friend to youth group."

Have everyone focus on the strong tree they chose earlier. Pray: **God, help us be like these trees along the shore. Keep us rooted deep in your Word and your love for us. Water us with your love, and help us bear fruit by reaching out to others. In Jesus' name, amen.**

12 Children's Home

Theme:
Childlike qualities

Scripture to Go: Mark 10:13-15
Some people brought their little children to Jesus so he could touch them, but his followers told them to stop. When Jesus saw this, he was upset and said to them, "Let the little children come to me. Don't stop them, because the kingdom of God belongs to people who are like these children. I tell you the truth, you must accept the kingdom of God as if you were a little child, or you will never enter it."

Devotion to Go

Arrange with the children's home administrators for your group to come and play with the children. Help with arts and crafts, snack time, music and games. Have kids lead games they enjoyed as children—Hopscotch, Marbles, Jacks, Kick-the-Can, Hide-and-Seek. After your time with the children, gather in a circle outside.

Ask: **How did you feel playing games you played as a child? How was playing these games like becoming a child again? What do you miss most about being a child? What are some childlike qualities you noticed in playing with these children today?**

Have someone in your group read aloud Mark 10:13-15. Ask: **Why would Jesus say his kingdom belongs to people** who're like children? What childlike qualities have you noticed today that would support Jesus' statement? If you could regain one childlike quality in your life, which one would you want? Say: God wants us all to be like the children we played with today—full of fun and life, and ready to trust God all the time.

Tell the person on your right a childlike quality you appreciate in him or her. For example, "I appreciate your playfulness." Then ask that person to tell the person on his or her right one childlike quality that's evident in that person's life. For example, "I like how you don't let anything get you down for long." Continue around the circle until everyone has had a chance.

Pray: Help us learn to be children again, God. Let each day bring us joy we can share with others. Help us walk in the light of your love. In Jesus' name, amen.

13 Choir Trip

Theme: Spreading God's love

Scripture to Go: Psalm 33:1-3

Sing to the Lord, you who do what is right; honest people should praise him. Praise the Lord on the harp; make music for him on a ten-stringed lyre. Sing a new song to him; play well and joyfully.

Devotion to Go

Sometime before your first performance, gather for this devotion.

Ask: **What's your favorite Christian song?** Sing a song that several kids name. Ask: **What's your favorite mainstream song? Does the love described in secular music sometimes remind you of God's love? Why or why not?**

Have the person sitting on your right read aloud Psalm 33: 1-3. Tell kids to work in pairs or trios and write a new Christian song based on a familiar tune. Encourage them to write a song about what God is doing in their lives right now.

Sing the new tunes, then ask: **How do you feel about your new song? How is writing and singing a new song like spreading God's love to new people? What's one "new song" God has given you to sing in your life during this trip? How can you spread the message of that song to others this week?**

Say: **As we sing this week, let's focus on finding new**

ways to spread God's love to others—both within our group and to those who listen to us.

Close with this prayer: **God, we pray for our music to touch the hearts of all who** **attend our concerts. Help us spread your love in new ways this week. Help us use our talents to the best of our abilities and to your glory. In Jesus' name, amen.**

14 Christian Concert

Theme: Reaching out to others

Scripture to Go: Ephesians 5:18-20
Do not be drunk with wine, which will ruin you, but be filled with the Spirit. Speak to each other with psalms, hymns, and spiritual songs, singing and making music in your hearts to the Lord. Always give thanks to God the Father for everything, in the name of our Lord Jesus Christ.

Devotion to Go

Gather in a group during an intermission (or before the concert) for this devotion. Tell kids they're going to have a devotion about reaching out to others. But first they get to experience it.

Form pairs. Have pairs each go meet one new person, introduce themselves and say what they've liked about the concert so far.

After five minutes, gather everyone together and ask: **How did it feel meeting new people? How is this like reaching out to others with God's love? How can we reach out to others at school? at work? at home?**

Have the person who was most enthused about the "reach-out" experience read aloud Ephesians 5:18-20. Ask: **Why are we told to speak to each other with songs and music? How do the songs you've heard so far make you feel about God? How are songs and music** good ways to reach out to others?

Brainstorm several ways kids can use this concert experience to reach out to others this week. For example, they can tell their non-Christian friends what happened at the concert or give one of the performer's tapes to a friend.

Close by praying: **Dear God, help us reach out to others this week and reflect the joy and love of the music we hear at this concert. In Jesus' name, amen.**

15 Community Recreation Center

Theme: Health

Scripture to Go: Acts 3:1-8
One day Peter and John went to the Temple at three o'clock, the time set each day for afternoon prayer service. There, at the Temple gate called Beautiful Gate, was a man who had been crippled all his life. Every day he was carried to this gate to beg for money from the people going into the Temple. The man saw Peter and John going into the Temple and asked them for money. Peter and John looked straight at him and said, "Look at us!" The man looked at them, thinking they were going to give him some money. But Peter said, "I don't have any silver or gold, but I do have something else I can give you. By the power of Jesus Christ from Nazareth, stand up and walk!" Then Peter took the man's right hand and lifted him up. Immediately the man's feet and ankles became strong. He jumped up, stood on his feet, and began to walk. He went into the Temple with them, walking and jumping and praising God.

Devotion to Go

After you've had time to swim, play basketball or volleyball, lift weights, or do whatever the center offers, meet outside on a grassy area.

Form two teams and run a relay race. Have one member of each team run up to a tree, run around it twice, do five jumping jacks, run back to his or her team and tag the next person, who then repeats the same exercises. The first team done wins. After the race, ask: **How did it feel to run the relay? How is that feeling like the joy or frustration of trying to stay healthy?**

Have the last person who shared read aloud Acts 3:1-8. Let kids each describe a time when an injury or illness kept them down. Ask: **What was it like not to do the activities you usually do? How did you feel when you were healed from the injury or illness?**

Form a circle, then go around the circle and tell kids each to name an ability they're thankful for, such as the ability to swim, play basketball or exercise. Go around once more. Have kids each share one goal for improving their health such as eat a balanced diet, exercise daily and get plenty of rest, or one goal for reaching a future sports achievement such as win a conference basketball championship.

Read aloud Acts 3:6-8. After each sentence is read, have kids stand up, say "Shape us up, Lord," and sit back down. Then pray: **Help us remember, God, that each one of us is only "temporarily abled" and that we should never take our health and abilities for granted. Help us take good care of our health. In Jesus' name, amen.**

16 Cross-country Skiing

Theme: Sin and forgiveness

Scripture to Go: Psalm 51:7-12
Take away my sin, and I will be clean. Wash me, and I will be whiter than snow. Make me hear sounds of joy and gladness; let the bones you crushed be happy again. Turn your face from my sins and wipe out all my guilt. Create in me a pure heart, God, and make my spirit right again. Do not send me away from you or take your Holy Spirit away from me. Give me back the joy of your salvation. Keep me strong by giving me a willing spirit.

Devotion to Go

After you've skied a while, take a break and enjoy some hot chocolate or cider while you have a devotion.

Look all around at the sparkling white snow and the goodness of God's creation. Ask kids to name adjectives that describe snow (white, clean, sparkling, and so on). Have someone who's wearing white read aloud Psalm 51:7-12. Say: **David wrote this Psalm and asked God to wash away his sin and he'd be clean, whiter than snow.** Ask: **Why is that a good definition of forgiveness?**

Have kids each make a snowball and hold it. Say: **Think about a time you did something wrong. Imagine the snowball represents that event. As a group, let's form a** cross shape with our snow-balls.

Ask: How did it feel to shape your "sin" snowballs into a cross? How is making the cross like when God forgives us? How do you feel when you are forgiven?

Have kids each grab a handful of snow and make another snowball. Say: Imagine this snowball represents all your past sins. Throw it as far away into the white distance as you can.

(*Pause while kids do this*) Then say: God forgives you of all your sins, so they can't be seen anymore. He washes you whiter than this snow.

As kids cross-country ski some more, suggest they say a personal prayer thanking God for his forgiveness. With each stride of their skiing, have them say these words: "Thank...you... God...I'm...forgiven."

17 Downhill Skiing

Theme: God's protection

Scripture to Go: Psalm 121:1-8

I look up to the hills, but where does my help come from? My help comes from the Lord, who made heaven and earth. He will not let you be defeated. He who guards you never sleeps. He who guards Israel never rests of sleeps. The Lord guards you. The Lord is the shade that protects you from the sun. The sun cannot hurt you during the day, and the moon cannot hurt you at night. The Lord will protect you from all dangers; he will guard your life. The Lord will guard you as you come and go, both now and forever.

Devotion to Go

Gather at the top of a peak. Ski areas usually have a burger bar on a mountaintop. Have kids get something to eat. Then gather in a sunny area on the porch, and look out over the mountains.

Ask kids how they feel when they look at the scenery. Let kids describe what they see by using each letter of the alphabet. For example, amazing, beautiful, creative, dynamic, evergreen, and so on.

Read aloud Psalm 121 as they look at the spectacular view.

Have everyone feel the sun's rays beating down on their skin. Say: **Imagine the sun's rays are different dangers or hurtful situations you face every day—arguments with friends or family, drugs, alcohol,** problems in school. Name other dangers you face. (*Pause and let kids name other dangers they face. Go to a shady area on the porch.*) The passage says "The Lord guards you. The Lord is the shade that protects you from the sun." Ask: How do you feel under the shade? How is this shade like God's protection? How does he protect us every day? How's the awesomeness of the mountains an assurance God can take care of us? When have you felt God's protection recently? How do you feel knowing that God protects you, and he never sleeps?

Have kids each think of one potentially hurtful or dangerous situation they face in their daily life. Say: When our lives seem out of control, remember that "The Lord will protect you from all dangers; he will guard your life. The Lord will guard you as you come and go, both now and forever."

Pray: The mountains are an awesome reminder of your power, God. Help us always trust in your protection. In Jesus' name, amen.

18 Fishing

Theme: Sharing your faith

Scripture to Go: Luke 5:4b, 6-11

[Jesus] said to Simon, "Take the boat into deep water, and put your nets in the water to catch some fish."

When the fishermen did as Jesus told them, they caught so many fish that the nets began to break. They called to their partners in the other boat to come and help them. They came and filled both boats so full that they were almost sinking.

When Simon Peter saw what had happened, he bowed down before Jesus and said, "Go away from me, Lord. I am a sinful man!" He and the other fishermen were amazed at the many fish they caught, as were James and John, the sons of Zebedee, Simon's partners.

Jesus said to Simon, "Don't be afraid. From now on you will fish for people." When the men brought their boats to the shore, they left everything and followed Jesus.

Devotion to Go

Do this devotion in boats or on the shore—wherever you decide to fish. Wait until several people have caught fish.

Ask: **For those of you who caught fish, how do you feel? How is this like how you feel when someone you share your faith with becomes a Christian? For those of you who didn't catch any fish yet, how do you feel? How is this** like the way you feel when a non-Christian friend doesn't choose to believe in Christ?

Have one person who has caught a fish read aloud Luke 5:4b, 6-11. Ask: **When was a time you tried really hard at something, but came up empty, like the disciples? If you'd been Simon Peter, how would you have felt when Jesus told him to try it one more time?**

Pass around a fish hook and ask: **How does a fish hook catch a fish? How can we be better "fishers of people" as a youth group? as individuals? as a church? What "hooks" can we use?**

After each of the following sentences, have kids say: "Let down your nets—try one more time":

● **When we feel discouraged about failing at making friends . . .**

● **When we have tried to follow Jesus, but we keep messing up . . .**

● **When a friend turns down an invitation to come to youth group . . .**

● **When a friend laughs at our relationships with Jesus . . .**

Pray: **God, you have called us to be fishers of men and women. Help us be alert for daily opportunities to share our faith. When we get discouraged, remind us to "let down our nets" one more time. In Jesus' name, amen.**

Have a fish fry with the fish kids catch. Talk more about practical ways to help others learn about Christ.

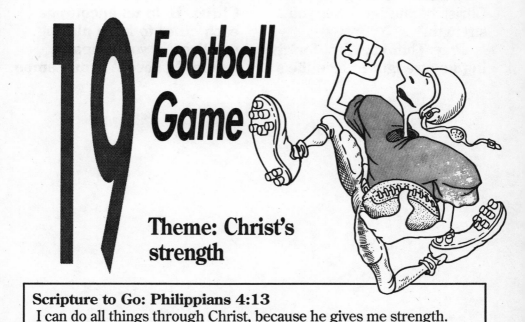

Football Game

Theme: Christ's strength

Scripture to Go: Philippians 4:13
I can do all things through Christ, because he gives me strength.

Devotion to Go

Gather at halftime on a grassy area for a devotion. Bring out a football and play catch for a while. Then set the football on the ground and gather kids in a circle around it.

Ask: **What can this football do by itself? What can the football do in the hands of an expert quarterback? How is your life like a football? How is Christ like an expert quarterback? Why do we sometimes resist God when he wants to direct our lives? How can we place our lives in his hands, like a football in the hands of a quarterback?**

Have someone read aloud Philippians 4:13. Say: **We can do anything through Christ who gives us the energy, wisdom, strength and power. Think of a "touchdown" time in your life—a time when Christ's strength got you through.**

After everyone has shared, toss the football to someone in the circle. Have that person name one area of his or her life to place in Christ's hands. Then have that person toss the football to someone else. Continue around the circle. After each person shares, have all kids respond in unison:

"You can do all things through Christ, because he gives you strength."

Pray: **Thanks, God, for giving us strength to face life's ups and downs through Christ. Help us encourage each other to keep placing our lives in your capable hands. In Jesus' name, amen.**

20

Hayride

Theme:
Praising God

Scripture to Go: Psalm 147:1, 4-11

Praise the Lord! It is good to sing praises to our God; it is good and pleasant to praise him...He counts the stars and names each one. Our Lord is great and very powerful. There is no limit to what he knows. The Lord defends the humble, but he throws the wicked to the ground. Sing praises to the Lord; praise our God with harps. He fills the sky with clouds and sends rain to the earth and makes grass grow on the hills. He gives food to cattle and to the little birds that call. He does not enjoy the strength of a horse or the strength of a man. The Lord is pleased with those who respect him, with those who trust his love.

Devotion to Go

During the hayride, sing songs such as "He's Everything to Me," "How Majestic Is Your Name," or "This Is the Day." After the hayride, gather around an open fire for the devotion. Or, if you don't want to make a fire, stay on the wagon for the devotion. Read aloud Psalm 147:1, 4-11.

Ask everyone to grab a piece of hay or blade of grass. Have kids each place it between their thumbs and try to blow through it, like a whistle. See who can make the loudest noise. Ask: **How did it feel to discover this ordinary grass could make music? How is whistling on the grass like God "drawing out" praise in your life?**

According to the passage I just read, what are some ways God draws praise out of his creation? out of you? How can we praise God more in our lives?

Roast marshmallows on sticks. Have kids each roast an extra marshmallow and give it to someone on the other side of the fire from them. As they give away the treat, have them say, "I praise God for you, because..."

For example, "I praise God for you because of your thoughtfulness," or "I praise God for you because of your beautiful singing voice."

Close by joining hands in a circle. Let kids pray silently as you say: **For your help as we try to praise you more, we ask you, Lord.** Ask everyone to squeeze in a giant group hug as an "amen."

21

Hiking

Theme: Past mistakes

Scripture to Go: Philippians 3:12-14

I do not mean that I am already as God wants me to be. I have not yet reached that goal, but I continue trying to reach it and to make it mine. Christ wants me to do that, which is the reason he made me his. Brothers and sisters, I know that I have not yet reached that goal, but there is one thing I always do. Forgetting the past and straining toward what is ahead, I keep trying to reach the goal and get the prize for which God called me through Christ to the life above.

Devotion to Go

Take a break from hiking. Ask everyone to search the area for a stick to write with. Once everyone has found one, ask kids to find a spot on the ground where they'll be comfortable.

Say: **Don't answer this question out loud—just think about it. What is a regret— something from your past— that you tend to kick yourself** for? (*Pause*) **How do you feel about this memory? Use your stick to write your regret or draw a symbol of it on the ground. We won't share as a large group, so be truthful.**

Read aloud Philippians 3:12-14. Ask: **How do you feel after hearing this passage? Why should we forget the past?** Say: Now, **take your stick and scratch out the thing you're** sorry for. Ask: **How does wip-**

ing out your regret make you feel? How is erasing your regret from the ground like leaving your past behind? How can we do that in real life?

Ask kids each to draw a symbol on the ground of their life's goal as a Christian. Ask: How is drawing this new goal in place of your past regret like "forgetting the past and straining toward what is ahead"? What seems to keep you from reaching your goal? How can we overcome those obstacles?

Take all your sticks and spell the word "Jesus." Gather in a circle around it and join hands while you pray: Dear God, thanks for your love. Help us follow Christ's goal for our lives and leave the past behind. Help us press on to be the kind of followers you've called us to be. In Jesus' name, amen.

Have everyone look to the goal of finishing your hike. At the end of the hike offer a reward such as Gatorade or cool fruit juices.

22 Horseback Riding

Theme: Receiving correction

Scripture to Go: Psalm 32:8-9
The Lord says, "I will make you wise and show you where to go. I will guide you and watch over you. So don't be like a horse or donkey, that doesn't understand. They must be led with bits and reins, or they will not come near you."

Devotion to Go

Go to a stable where horses are kept and supplied for recreational riders. Ask the horseback riding guide to help kids experiment with the reins. Have kids see where the horse goes when they pull to the right, pull to the left or pull back. Let them see what happens when they don't do anything with the reins.

After the ride, find a quiet spot and gather everyone together. Ask someone who is an experienced horseback rider to read aloud Psalm 32:8-9. Ask: **How did you experience this "stubborn-horse" truth in the ride today? How did it feel to have your horse respond to your steering? How was directing your horse like God's direction in your life? What are some "reins" God has in your life? When have you been like the stubborn donkey mentioned in this passage?**

Tell kids you're going to help them think of a way to learn from correction, not get angry with it. Ask them to respond silently

49

when you pause—they don't need to share in a large group.

Say: **Everyone consider a recent reprimand or time you were corrected.** (*Pause*) **How did you feel?** (*Pause*) **Was there** *any* **truth to the need for correcting?** (*Pause*) **How can you learn from the situation?** (*Pause*)

Ask: **What steps did we just follow? How did the steps help you as you thought about a recent reprimand?**

Say: **Whenever you're corrected in the future, rather than get angry, ask yourself if there's any truth in the correction and how you can learn from it.**

Pray: **It feels good to be able to steer our horses, God. May we also be as willing to be steered by your Spirit and the wise counsel of those who love us. In Jesus' name, amen.**

23 Ice Cream Parlor

Theme: Watching your words

> **Scripture to Go: Proverbs 17:27-28**
> The smart person says very little, and one with understanding stays calm. Even fools seem to be wise if they keep quiet; if they don't speak, they appear to understand.

Devotion to Go

Have a race to see who can take the most bites of ice cream in 10 seconds. Congratulate the winner, then ask: **What happens when you eat your ice cream too quickly? How is eating your ice cream too fast like being the kind of person who speaks without thinking?**

Read aloud Proverbs 17:27-28. Ask: **What does this passage say about the importance of keeping your tongue "on ice" or under control? How does** "quietness" **make a person seem wise? What are some ways we can better control what we say?**

Say: **Learning to control what you say can not only make you appear wise, it can keep you out of trouble and prevent you from hurting others with careless words.**

Pray: **Dear God, help us stay "cool" in life's tough situations and control how we speak to others. In Jesus' name, amen.**

24 Ice Skating

Theme: Busyness

Scripture to Go: Luke 10:38-42

While Jesus and his followers were traveling, Jesus went into a town. A woman named Martha let Jesus stay at her house. Martha had a sister named Mary, who was sitting at Jesus' feet and listening to him teach. But Martha was busy with all the work to be done. She went in and said, "Lord, don't you care that my sister has left me alone to do all the work? Tell her to help me."

But the Lord answered her, "Martha, Martha, you are worried and upset about many things. Only one thing is important. Mary has chosen the better thing, and it will never be taken away from her."

Devotion to Go

Give kids three minutes to try as many ice-skating tricks as they can—skate backward, hold hands with a partner and skate in a circle, skate on one foot.

Stop for a break and read aloud Luke 10:38-42. Ask: **How did you feel balancing on the blades? How did you feel doing so many ice-skating tricks in a short period of time? Which is easier—skating along normally or trying all these fancy tricks? How is doing tricks on your ice skates like trying to balance a busy, hectic schedule? How are our tricks like Martha's attitude in this passage? How are we like Martha? Mary?**

Read aloud the following questions. Have kids stand up if their answer is "I'm balancing." Have them sit down if their answer is "I've lost my balance." Ask: **How's your balance between Bible reading and television watching? How's your balance between time talking to God in prayer and time talking to friends on the phone? How's your balance between investing time at church and investing time on yourself?**

Tell kids to think about how they might change their lives to be more like Mary in the passage. Ask: **What one activity can you get out of so you can have more time with God?** Have kids each tell their answer to a person sitting close to them.

Pray: **We, like Martha, get worried and upset and preoccupied with so many things that aren't really that important. Help us be more like Mary and remember "only one thing is important"—to spend time with you, God. In Jesus name, amen.**

Encourage kids to think about their busy-balancing-act goal as they go back to balancing on their skates.

25 Kite Flying

Theme: Death and heaven

Scripture to Go: 1 Thessalonians 4:13-18

Brothers and sisters, we want you to know about those Christians who have died so you will not be sad, as others who have no hope. We believe that Jesus died and that he rose again. So, because of him, God will raise with Jesus those who have died. What we tell you now is the Lord's own message. We who are living when the Lord comes again will not go before those who have already died. The Lord himself will come down from heaven with a loud command, with the voice of the archangel, and with the trumpet call of God. And those who have died believing in Christ will rise first. After that, we who are still alive will be gathered up with them in the clouds to meet the Lord in the air. And we will be with the Lord forever. So encourage each other with these words.

Devotion to Go

Go to a kite festival, or host your own. Provide kids with inexpensive kites. At a high point during the day, hold a contest to see who can fly their kite the highest. When the kites have gone as high as they can, have kids let go of their strings. Allow time for kids to gather their kites (if they can find them!), then gather everyone together.

Ask: **How did it feel to fly your kites so high? How did you feel letting them go? How** is flying your kite so high like people trying to get to heaven? When you let the strings go, did the kites "take off" into outer space? Why not? How is that like what happens when people try to make their own way to heaven?

Ask a person who flew his or her kite the highest to read aloud 1 Thessalonians 4:13-18. Ask: **What does this passage tell us about death for Christians? about heaven? How was flying your kite so high like Christians living in the world?**

What are some "strings" that hold you to life down here? What are you looking forward to about heaven? Until the day we get to go to heaven, how can we live our lives like high-flying kites?

Before you start flying the kites again, say this prayer: **We forget, God, that this life is just a "foretaste of the feast to come." May your blessings here build our anticipation of spending eternity with you. Thanks for giving us hope of living forever with you. In Jesus' name, amen.**

26 Miniature Golf

Theme: Fruit of the Spirit

Scripture to Go: Galatians 5:22-26
But the Spirit produces the fruit of love, joy, peace, patience, kindness, goodness, faithfulness, gentleness, self-control. There is no law that says these things are wrong. Those who belong to Christ Jesus have crucified their own sinful selves. They have given up their old selfish feelings and the evil things they wanted to do. We get our new life from the Spirit, so we should follow the Spirit. We must not be proud or make trouble with each other or be jealous of each other.

Devotion to Go

Gather at the starting point of the miniature golf course. Distribute pencils and the score cards. Tell kids they're going to talk about the fruit of the Spirit as they play golf. Ask a person who's standing close to you to read aloud Galatians 5:22-26.

If you're playing nine holes, have kids write one fruit of the Spirit by each hole on their score cards. If you're playing 18 holes, have kids write one fruit of the Spirit next to every two holes on their score cards.

Play golf in pairs. Have partners discuss the following questions for each fruit at its assigned hole(s): **Are you weak or strong in this fruit of the Spirit? What's one way you could strengthen this fruit in your life?**

When the kids finish their

games of miniature golf, have partners discuss the obstacles, hazards or booby traps in the course. Ask: **Which obstacle was the most difficult? How did you feel as you tried to overcome that obstacle? How's that obstacle like something that keeps you from showing a fruit of the Spirit in your life? How was overcoming that obstacle on the course like overcoming the obstacles in our lives that keep us from walking by God's Spirit?**

Say: **This week, let's all focus on one fruit of the Spirit that we need to develop in our lives and work on overcoming the obstacles that keep that fruit from growing.**

Pray: **Help us, God, to be "fruitful" in our lives. When we feel tempted to turn away from you, help us make the choice to walk by your Spirit. In Jesus' name, amen.**

27 Movie

Theme:
Friendship

Scripture to Go: Ecclesiastes 4:9-12
Two people are better than one, because they get more done by working together. If one falls down, the other can help him up. But it is bad for the person who is alone and falls, because no one is there to help. If two lie down together, they will be warm, but a person alone will not be warm. An enemy might defeat one person, but two people together can defend themselves; a rope that is woven of three strings is hard to break.

Devotion to Go

See the movie first. Ask kids to keep their ticket stubs for the devotion. Go outside (if the weather is nice) or back to the church for the devotion.

Form small groups, and have each group choose a scene from the movie to re-enact. Afterward, ask: **How did it feel to act out a scene from the movie? How was acting out your scene like** being a real movie star? **What's great about being a movie star? How are we like movie stars to our friends? How is friendship like stardom? How is it different?**

Read aloud Ecclesiastes 4: 9-12. Ask: **When you "fall down," how have your friends helped you up? How do friends help you face the "cold" circumstances of life? How do friends defend each** other? Why are "two better than one"? After reading this passage, which would you rather have next to you in life—a movie star or a friend? Explain.

Ask kids each to form partners with a person sitting on either side of them. Say: **On the back of your ticket stub, in tiny letters, write one thing you'll do for your partner this week to help him or her as a friend. Give the ticket stub to that person as a reminder.**

As a closing, have a "blessing" time when kids can "shake hands with the stars." Tell kids to affirm each other by shaking hands with one another and saying: "You're a real star to me because..." Have kids complete the statement for each person they shake hands with.

Pray: **God, help us always remember "what a friend we have in Jesus." Make us alert to opportunities for reaching out to others. Thanks, God, for our "star-quality friends." In Jesus' name, amen.**

28 Museum

Theme: Self-esteem

Scripture to Go: Psalm 139:13-16
You made my whole being; you formed me in my mother's body. I praise you because you made me in an amazing and wonderful way. What you have done is wonderful. I know this very well. You saw my bones being formed as I took shape in my mother's body. When I was put together there, you saw my body as it was formed. All the days planned for me were written in your book before I was one day old.

Devotion to Go

When you enter the museum, get a brochure for each person. Walk through the museum and enjoy the exhibits. Have kids think about the value of the items behind various glass cases.

About halfway through your tour, pull kids aside. Talk about all the treasures you've seen in the museum. Have a volunteer read aloud Psalm 139:13-16.

On their brochures, have kids each draw a simple "exhibit" of their lives. Have them draw or describe a "treasure" they gained during each time period of their lives; for example, "infancy"—parents holding them, "toddler years"—a new baby sister, "early elementary"—a favorite toy, "later elementary"—a favorite teacher, "junior high"—a best friend, "high school"—a favorite sport.

Let kids explain their personal exhibits, then ask: **How did you feel creating your personal exhibit? How did you feel telling others about it? How is that feeling like the feeling God has about the treasures he's placed in your life? How is it different? How does knowing that God created you in such a wonderful way change the way you see yourself?**

Reread the passage. Emphasize that God knew what he was doing in each of their lives. And he planned it very well!

Pray: **What good news, God! To think of you being so intimately involved in our lives. Even when bad things happen, we can know that it's all going to turn out for good, because you love us. Forgive us when we get uptight and feel sad about ourselves. Help us see ourselves through your loving eyes. In Jesus' name, amen.**

Continue touring the museum, viewing exhibits and noticing God's love expressed throughout time.

29 Nursing Home

Theme:
Wisdom

Scripture to Go: Proverbs 23:12
Remember what you are taught, and listen carefully to words of knowledge.

Devotion to Go

Arrange with a local nursing home for your group to come visit, have a devotion in a lounge and interview residents. Ask the director for a list of residents' names who would like to be interviewed.

Arrive at the nursing home, and gather in the lounge for a quick devotion. Ask for a volunteer to read aloud Proverbs 23:12. Ask: **Who are teachers in our lives? Why's it sometimes hard to listen to teachers, parents and grandparents**
when they give us advice? How can we learn from them, even if we don't like the advice they give us?** Say: **We're going to take time to open our ears to words of wisdom by interviewing some residents.**

Form pairs. Assign each partner a resident to interview. Kids can jot down the residents' answers or tape record the interviews. Partners can use these questions:

● Describe a favorite memory when you were a teenager. What advice would you give to help us make the most out of our youth?

● Describe a favorite school memory. What advice would you give to help us gain the most knowledge from school?

● Describe a favorite family memory. What advice would you give to help us have a happy family?

Afterward, gather in the lounge or back at your church. Share the advice kids received. Ask: **How did you feel interviewing the residents? How was interviewing them like gaining wisdom in life? How else can you "remember what you are taught, and listen** **carefully to words of knowledge"?**

On their interview sheets or tape recorders, have kids record one way they'll strive to gain more wisdom in life, starting today.

Give thanks for the wisdom received by praying: **Dear God, we give thanks for the wisdom of the ages, especially for the wisdom gathered today. Help all of us to be willing to learn from one another. In Jesus' name, amen.**

30 Picnic

Theme:
Spiritual growth

Scripture to Go: 2 Peter 1:5-8
Because you have these blessings, do your best to add these things to your lives: to your faith, add goodness; and to your goodness, add knowledge; and to your knowledge; add self-control; and to your self-control, add patience; and to your patience, add service for God; and to your service for God, add kindness for your brothers and sisters in Christ; and to this kindness, add love. If these things are in you and are growing, they will help you to be useful and productive in your knowledge of our Lord Jesus Christ.

Devotion to Go

Go on a picnic. Set out the supplies to make super-duper sandwiches. Hold a contest to see who can make the thickest sandwich. The only rule is that they must eat what they create.

When everyone is finished, measure the sandwiches and congratulate the winner. As kids consume their creations, ask: **What was fun about building such a huge sandwich? What was difficult about it? How does adding extras on a sandwich make it taste better?**

Read aloud 2 Peter 1:5-8. Ask: **How's building a huge sandwich like "building up" your spiritual life? How's it different? What's fun about building up your spiritual life? What's difficult about it? How** does focusing on your spiritual life make everything in life better?

Go through the passage again, and ask kids to give practical examples of ways to "add" the qualities in the passage to their lives. Ask: **If the list in this passage represents a progressive process of spiritual growth, where are you in the process? What's the next step you need to take to grow spiritually?**

Have kids each choose one thing they'll do this week to begin to work on building up their spiritual lives.

Pray: **God, thank you for these great sandwiches we've built. And thank you, too, for showing us how to build our spiritual lives so we can be strong followers of Jesus. Help us follow the path of growth you've set before us. In Jesus' name, amen.**

31 Pizza Restaurant

Theme: Coming to Christ

Scripture to Go: Luke 14:16b-24

"A man gave a big banquet and invited many people. When it was time to eat, the man sent his servant to tell the guests, 'Come. Everything is ready.'

"But all the guests made excuses. The first one said, 'I have just bought a field, and I must go look at it. Please excuse me.' Another said, 'I have just bought five pairs of oxen; I must go and try them. Please excuse me.' A third person said, 'I just got married; I can't come.' So the servant returned and told his master what had happened. Then the master became angry and said, 'Go at once into the streets and alleys of the town, and bring in the poor, the crippled, the blind, and the lame.' Later the servant said to him, 'Master, I did what you commanded, but we still have room.' The master said to the servant, 'Go out to the roads and country lanes, and urge the people there to come so my house will be full. I tell you, none of those whom I invited first will eat with me.' "

Devotion to Go

Prior to this devotion, ask the restaurant management to serve your food late and give your group several silly excuses for why it's late. For example, "I'm sorry. Your food is late because we got caught up watching television in the back," or "I'm sorry. You're food is late because the cook tripped me. I fired him."

Come up with three or four excuses the restaurant can use.

Go to the restaurant. Order your food. Watch kids' reactions as the staff comes to them with their excuses. Finally when you get your food, let kids in on the setup and ask: **How did you feel as you heard all the excuses? What did you want to do by the time we heard the third or fourth excuse?**

Read Luke 14:16b-24, then ask: **How is the way we felt about the excuses like the way God felt in this passage? How was his reaction similar to ours? What does the banquet represent? Who might miss out on the great heavenly feast? What excuses do people make for not coming to Christ? What attitude do you think is at the heart of all those excuses?**

Tell everyone to find some item on the table and use it to represent an "excuse" for not coming to Jesus. For example, someone could hold up a salt-shaker and say, "I can't come to Jesus right now. I've made some good food and got a lot of friends coming over for a party." Another person could pick up a napkin and say, "Sorry. I don't have time to come to Jesus right now. I just heard about a good sale on napkins. I have to go and buy several boxes before they run out."

Ask: **If Jesus were to ask you to come to him right now, what things in your life might tempt you to put him off?** Go around the table and let kids each tell one thing they'll remove from their lives that keeps them from coming to Jesus.

Pray: **Dear God, our excuses are weak. Help us always be ready to come to you and do the work of your kingdom. In Jesus name, amen.**

32 Rafting

Theme: Fear

Scripture to Go: Luke 8:22-25

One day Jesus and his followers got into a boat, and he said to them, "Let's go across the lake." And so they started across. While they were sailing, Jesus fell asleep. A very strong wind blew up on the lake, causing the boat to fill with water, and they were in danger.

The followers went to Jesus and woke him, saying, "Master! Master! We will drown!"

Jesus got up and gave a command to the wind and the waves. They stopped, and it became calm. Jesus said to his followers, "Where is your faith?"

The followers were afraid and amazed and said to each other, "Who is this that commands even the wind and the water, and they obey him?"

Devotion to Go

Enjoy the rapids. Do this devotion when you've pulled over to the shore for a break or for lunch.

Ask: **How did you feel as you rode the rapids today?**

What experience today made you afraid—even a little? How did you handle your fear? What helped you overcome your fear? How is that like the way you deal with fear in real life?

Have the person with the

wettest hair read aloud Luke 8:22-25. Ask: **How is your fear similar or different to the fear the disciples must have felt in this story? What are some "sinking problems" you fear in day-to-day living? What helps you deal with your fear in those situations? Based on this passage, what might Jesus tell you about your fears? How should we respond to God when we are afraid?** Say: **Like the disciples went to Jesus for help, we can go to Jesus for help with all** our fears. **Jesus is like this life jacket. He holds us close and saves us from the fears that surround us.**

Pass around a life jacket. Ask kids each to hold the life jacket and say one thing they fear. As each person shares, have the rest of the group say: "Jesus is our safety. He saves us from all we fear." Close by praying: **God, thank you for sending Jesus to deliver us from all our fears. Help us place our trust in you when we are afraid. In Jesus' name, amen.**

33 Roller Skating

**Theme:
Correcting others**

Scripture to Go: Galatians 6:1-5

Brothers and sisters, if someone in your group does something wrong, you who are spiritual should go to that person and gently help make him right again. But be careful, because you might be tempted to sin, too. By helping each other with your troubles, you truly obey the law of Christ. If anyone thinks he is important when he really is not, he is only fooling himself. Each person should judge his own actions and not compare himself with others. Then he can be proud for what he himself has done. Each person must be responsible for himself.

Devotion to Go

Roller skate until it seems everyone is ready to take a break. Find a table or two, and have everyone gather around. Ask: **What's difficult about roller skating? How did you first learn how to roller skate?**

Did your friends help you learn? How have you helped each other today out on the rink? How is that like the way you help each other in life?

Try a "helping friends" experiment. Ask one person to stand, then ask two others to stand on either side of the first person and face the opposite direction. Have all three link arms. The object is for the two to slowly skate forward, while the middle person is pulled along backward. Let everyone have a turn being the middle person pulled backward. Ask: **How did you feel being the middle person? Why did you have to trust the two on either side of you? How did it feel being the outside people? Why did you have to be careful as you skated with the person in the middle? How is this experience like the way we help each other in life? How is it like the way we help someone who's making poor choices in life?**

Have a volunteer read aloud Galatians 6:1-5. Ask: **What does this passage say about correcting a friend who may be making a mistake in life? How should we correct the person? What are things you see friends doing that are bad for them?**

Have kids each think of a friend who might need correcting. Have kids form pairs and discuss their situation. Remind kids to keep friends' names anonymous as they try to help each other with a positive way to deal with the situation.

Say: **Like in roller skating, when you fall down, a friend can pick you back up. When we see friends doing something potentially harmful, we can gently correct them, yet affirm them and their friendship at the same time.**

Pray: **God, help us watch out for each other and protect each other from the pitfalls we all face. Teach us how to be accountable as brothers and sisters in Christ. In Jesus' name, amen.**

34 Scavenger Hunt

Theme: Envy

> **Scripture to Go: Genesis 27:41**
> After that Esau hated Jacob because of the blessing from Isaac. He thought to himself, "My father will soon die, and I will be sad for him. Then I will kill Jacob."

Devotion to Go

Gather in your church before your scavenger hunt. Form teams and give each team a list of items to ask for as they walk around the neighborhood or to church members' homes. Race to see who can collect the most items on the list within a specific time.

Afterward, congratulate the winners. Ask: **How do you feel after the hunt? How do you feel knowing that other teams got more than your team?**

How are those feelings like envy? What makes you envious in daily life?

Say: **Jacob and Esau were brothers who were envious of each other. Jacob cheated Esau out of his father's blessing.** Ask a member from the team with the most items to read aloud Genesis 27:41. Ask: **Who's someone you've envied? Why did you envy that person? How was your envy like Esau's? What's wrong with comparing ourselves to others? How is comparing our- selves to others like compar-**

ing apples with oranges? How can we beat envy?

Say: **We're all equally special and unique in God's eyes. When we really understand that truth, we no longer feel the need to envy others, because we're happy with who we are and what we have.**

Give everyone a chance to bless each other by going on a "compliment scavenger hunt." On "go," have kids each find a partner and exchange as many compliments as they can. Blow a whistle or clap your hands after 10 seconds, then have kids find new partners and exchange compliments. Repeat this process until kids exchange compliments with a variety of people.

Pray: **Dear God, envy can poison our lives. Teach us to not compare ourselves to others. Help us give thanks for what we have, give thanks for others' gifts and abilities and reach out to others in love. In Jesus' name, amen.**

35

Service Trip

Theme: Reaching out to others

Scripture to Go: Mark 6:7-12

He called his twelve followers together and got ready to send them out two by two and gave them authority over evil spirits. This is what Jesus commanded them: "Take nothing for your trip except a walking stick. Take no bread, no bag, and no money in your pockets. Wear sandals, but take only the clothes you are wearing. When you enter a house, stay there until you leave that town. If the people in a certain place refuse to welcome you or listen to you, leave that place. Shake its dust off your feet as a warning to them." So the followers went out and preached that people should change their hearts and lives.

Devotion to Go

Wherever you go on a mission trip—to a workcamp, to fix a home for Habitat for Humanity, to fix a children's home or orphanage in Mexico—do this devotion your first day out.

Gather in a large room. Use the kids and the room to make a human map of the United States.

Point out the following positions:

● upper-left corner represents Washington state;

● upper-right corner represents Maine;

● lower-left corner represents California; and

● lower-right corner represents Florida.

Ask kids to stand in the place on the map that represents

where they were born or where they spent their childhood. If kids stand near the same place on the map, have them stand in the place their parents were born, or their grandparents.

Now have kids switch places with someone else on the map. Ask: **How would you feel if you'd been raised in your new location? How is this like the way you feel when going on a mission trip or doing a service for others?** Have everyone sit down. Ask a person who's a first-time "mission goer" to read aloud Mark 6:7-12. Ask: **How did Jesus prepare his disciples to go out on a mission? What does Jesus' example teach us about our own mission trip?**

Using Jesus' guidelines from the passage, have kids brainstorm a list of "service trip" guidelines for your group. Write the ideas on a piece of paper and review them every time you gather for devotions during your mission trip.

Pray: **The whole world is the mission field you've called us to, God. Help us be faithful to serve others in the way you want us to. In Jesus' name, amen.**

36

Shopping Mall

Theme: Possessions

Devotion to Go

Meet at a candy shop or discount store in a shopping mall. Tell kids you'll buy them each an item (under a dollar). After everyone has an item, say: **Now, your goal is to give your item to a shopper within the next 5 minutes.**

Give time for kids to do this, then gather for a devotion. Ask: **How did it feel to receive your item? How did it feel to give it away? How would you have felt if I'd asked you to give away something more valuable? How are these feelings like your attitudes toward your possessions? How does Jesus want us to feel about earthly possessions?**

Read aloud Mark 10:24b-27. Let kids observe their surroundings and name 10 items they would buy, if money were no object. Ask: **If you were rich, why would it be difficult to give up those possessions and follow Jesus?**

Ask group members to tell about their most prized possession, such as a car, bike or stereo. Ask: **How would you feel giving away your most prized possession and never replacing it? How do you think Jesus feels when we place a greater priority on our possessions than on doing his will? What kind of people seem "possessed by their possessions"?**

Have kids think of the lifestyle they hope to have someday. Ask: **How does it compare with the example Jesus gives in the passage? What's the good news in this passage?** Say: **With God, all things are possible. He can help us change our focus off of earthly possessions and on to his heavenly ones.**

Pray: **Forgive us, God, when we become possessed by our possessions. Help us seek first your kingdom—a treasure that will last forever. In Jesus' name, amen.**

37 Sledding or Tubing

Theme:
Teamwork

Scripture to Go: 1 Thessalonians 5:11
So encourage each other and give each other strength, just as you are doing now.

Devotion to Go

Form a tubing or sledding chain down the hill. Let kids experience teamwork by hanging on to each other.

When it's time for a break, ask: **What was fun about going down the hill in a chain? What was difficult about it?** Ask the person with the coldest nose to read 1 Thessalonians 5:11. Ask: **What elements of teamwork are described in this verse? What teams are you a part of in everyday life? How does encouragement help make teamwork flow? How can we improve the way we work together in this group?**

Form pairs and have them each build a snowman and decorate it with things that represent "teamwork" qualities, such as pebbles in the shape of a heart or twigs in the shape of a big smile. When everyone is finished, let pairs each explain their symbols.

Pray: **Dear God, what a treasure it is to work together. Help us learn to work together in love. In Jesus' name, amen.**

38 Soup Kitchen

Theme: Hot or cold faith

Scripture to Go: Revelation 3:15-16, 19-20

"I know what you do, that you are not hot or cold. I wish that you were hot or cold! But because you are lukewarm—neither hot, nor cold—I am ready to spit you out of my mouth...I correct and punish those whom I love. So be eager to do right, and change your hearts and lives. Here I am! I stand at the door and knock. If you hear my voice and open the door, I will come in and eat with you, and you will eat with me."

Devotion to Go

Arrange with the soup kitchen volunteers for your group to help prepare and serve a lunch or supper. Arrange to go earlier and have this devotion on the premises. Have kids each bring a can of soup to donate to the kitchen.

Open one can of soup (cream of mushroom works great!), pour it in a bowl, and have kids taste it without heating it up. Encourage them to taste the soup even if they don't want to. Ask: **Did you like the soup? Why or why not? What does the soup need to make it good food? How is tasting lukewarm soup like living a halfhearted Christian life? What does God think about people who have a "lukewarm" faith?**

Have someone who likes to cook read aloud Revelation 3:

15-16, 19-20. Ask: **Why does God want us to be either hot or cold with our faith? What temperature would you describe your faith? Explain. How could you "turn up the heat"? What are some bold ways we can increase our faith and show others God's love?**

Pray: **God, out of all the things in life we might be "turned on" to, let us be turned on to you and your love for everyone in our world—big or little, old or young, rich or poor. Thanks for loving us all. In Jesus' name, amen.**

Commend kids for their willingness to serve at the soup kitchen as a way to show their faith isn't lukewarm. Assign a couple of kids to the door to be greeters. Encourage kids to see Jesus in each person they welcome and serve today. Say: **Open the door, Jesus will eat with us, and we with him.**

39 Spelunking

Theme:
Resurrection

Scripture to Go: Matthew 28:1-7
The day after the Sabbath day was the first day of the week. At dawn on the first day, Mary Magdalene and another woman named Mary went to look at the tomb.

At that time there was a strong earthquake. An angel of the Lord came down from heaven, went to the tomb, and rolled the stone away from the entrance. Then he sat on the stone. He was shining as bright as lightning, and his clothes were white as snow. The soldiers guarding the tomb shook with fear because of the angel, and they became like dead men.

The angel said to the women, "Don't be afraid. I know that you are looking for Jesus, who has been crucified. He is not here. He has risen from the dead as he said he would. Come and see the place where his body was. And go quickly and tell his followers, 'Jesus has risen from the dead. He is going into Galilee ahead of you, and you will see him there.' " Then the angel said, "Now I have told you."

Devotion to Go

Explore the cave. At some point in your exploration, turn out all the lights, and let kids experience the near-total darkness.

Turn on the lights. Ask: **How does it feel to go into the cave? How do you feel with the lights turned out? How is that like how Jesus might've felt when he faced death?**

How is that like how you feel when you face different kinds of "death" in your own life; for example, the loss of a friend, failure at school, divorce?

Continue the cave exploration. After emerging from the depths, gather everyone in a circle.

Have someone who likes mountain climbing read aloud Matthew 28:1-7. Ask: **How did you feel as you entered the light of day again? How is that feeling like a resurrection? How do you think Jesus felt when he went from death to** life? **What kinds of "resurrection" might we experience in our lives? How was emerging from the cave like gaining new life? How can Jesus help you gain new life today?**

Ask kids to think of examples of sad things in their lives that feel dead to them. Ask: **How can Jesus bring a resurrection to these areas of your life? How can you help him do that?**

Pray: **God, hear us as we name some dark times we've faced lately** (*pause*). **Help us to know it doesn't stay dark forever. Come and bring new life to us today. In Jesus' name, amen.**

40 Star Watching

Theme: We are special

Scripture to Go: Psalm 8:3-9
I look at your heavens, which you made with your fingers. I see the moon and stars, which you created. But why are people important to you? Why do you take care of human beings? You made them a little lower than the angels and crowned them with glory and honor. You put them in charge of everything you made. You put all things under their control: all the sheep, the cattle, and the wild animals, the birds in the sky, the fish in the sea, and everything that lives under water. Lord our Lord, your name is the most wonderful name in all the earth!

Devotion to Go

Go to a planetarium or observatory, or borrow someone's telescope and do your own star watching. Find a grassy spot to lay on, and watch the stars and moon at night. Lay out a few blankets for kids to rest on.

Sing songs such as "How Majestic Is Thy Name," "How Great Thou Art" or "Blessed Be the Rock." Have kids each see if they can point out different star formations. Let them make up their own. Ask someone who loves astronomy to read aloud Psalm 8:3-9.

Have kids close their eyes, shut out the starlight and just see darkness. Say: **Think of a time when you felt like you weren't** important. It could've been when you didn't get a part in a play or when your parents didn't attend your choir concert or when a teacher didn't like your answer to a question he or she asked. How did you feel? How were your feelings like the darkness you see?

Have kids open their eyes and look at God's great creation. Read the passage again, emphasizing how important we are to God.

Ask: How do you feel after hearing the passage and looking at the stars? How important are you according to the passage? Why do you think you are so important to God?

Say: Sometimes we may feel so insignificant in comparison to the universe and all of God's creation. But he has crowned us all with glory and honor! What a compliment.

Go around and have kids each say one thing that makes the person on their right sparkling and special in God's sight. After everyone has received a compliment, pray: Our most creative God, when we feel insignificant and unimportant, help us remember the beauty of the stars and that you've crowned us with glory and honor. You made each one of us special and important. In Jesus' name, amen.

41

Study Nights

Theme: Education

Scripture to Go: Ecclesiastes 9:17-18
The quiet words of a wise person are better than the shouts of a foolish ruler. Wisdom is better than weapons of war, but one sinner can destroy much good.

Devotion to Go

After studying for about an hour, have kids take a devotion break. Go outside, form two teams and use a rope to play a few rounds of Tug of War. Congratulate the first team to win three times.

Ask: **How did your team do? How did your team change its methods each time you played? How was preparing for this "war" like getting an education at school? What happens when you don't prepare? What happens when you do?**

Have the person whose hands are the sorest read aloud Ecclesiastes 9:17-18.

Ask: **How do you feel about studying? Why do you think it's important? What good is an education in life? How is "wisdom better than weapons of war"? How can "one sinner destroy much good" in a school setting?**

Let kids create a "school" version of the passage by filling in the blanks:

_____of a wise _____ are better than_____of a foolish _____.

For example, "The studies of a wise student are better than the schemes of a foolish cheater," or "The thoughts of a wise teacher are better than the distractions of a foolish classmate." Conclude with this prayer: **Help us, God, to develop good study habits that might carry us through our whole life. Especially help us to faithfully study your Word—that we might be truly wise. In Jesus' name, amen.**

42 Swimming Pool

Theme: Overcoming problems

Scripture to Go: John 5:2-9
In Jerusalem there is a pool with five covered porches, which is called Bethzatha in the Jewish language. This pool is near the Sheep Gate. Many sick people were lying on the porches beside the pool. Some were blind, some were crippled, and some were paralyzed. A man was lying there who had been sick for thirty-eight years. When Jesus saw the man and knew that he had been sick for such a long time, Jesus asked him, "Do you want to be well?"

The sick man answered, "Sir, there is no one to help me get into the pool when the water starts moving. While I am coming to the water, someone else always gets in before me."

Then Jesus said, "Stand up. Pick up your mat and walk." And immediately the man was well; he picked up his mat and began to walk.

Devotion to Go

Bring a treat, such as a candy bar, to the pool. You'll also need a float to set it on. After kids swim for a while, gather by the pool's edge.

Tell the kids you're going to present them with a problem they must "overcome." Place the candy bar on the float and push it out toward the middle of the pool. Say: **The first person to get to the treat without getting wet or getting the treat wet can have it.**

If someone overcomes the problem, reward him or her with the treat. It's okay if no one comes up with a solution. Ask: **How did it feel to try to get to the treat? How is that like trying to solve "impossible" problems in our lives?** Say: **The Bible records a story of an impossible situation that one man faced. North of the Temple in Jerusalem, there was a pool of water. An angel was supposed to come down and stir the water from time to time. Whenever this happened, the first person in the pool was cured from any sickness he or she had.**

Ask a person with relatively dry hands to read aloud John 5: 2-9. Ask: **What excuse did the man give Jesus when he asked if he wanted to be cured? Do you think the man wanted to be cured? Why or why not? Why is it sometimes easier to live "status quo"**

and not be healed or helped? What are some "crippling" problems we face today? Why do some people use problems as excuses and other people achieve great things in spite of those same problems? Say: **Think of an emotional or inner hurt you'd like to be "cured" of.** Ask: **Why does your situation feel like it's impossible? What are some ways God could solve your problem, if you let him?**

Say: **God is there to help us when things get tough in life. With God's help, we can overcome our problems and help others do the same.** Pray: **God, help us never to hide behind our problems or feel like they're too big. Reveal your power within us to help us know that, with you, anything is possible. In Jesus' name, amen.**

43 Tennis

Theme: Love

Scripture to Go: 1 Corinthians 13:4-8a
Love is patient and kind. Love is not jealous, it does not brag, and it is not proud. Love is not rude, is not selfish, and does not get upset with others. Love does not count up wrongs that have been done. Love is not happy with evil but is happy with the truth. Love patiently accepts all things. It always trusts, always hopes, and always remains strong. Love never ends.

Devotion to Go

Play at least an hour of tennis with kids. Play with all the kids at some point during the time, even if you have to interrupt a game in progress. As you play, pretend to be cranky. Occasionally call your opponents' serves "out," even when they're "in." Watch kids' reactions to your wrong calls and bad attitude. At the end of your tennis time, gather in a circle on a nearby grassy area.

Ask: **What was fun about playing today? What wasn't fun about playing? How did you feel about the way I played today? How was dealing with my rudeness and bad attitude like choosing to love rather than hate? What does it mean to love?** Say: **We're going to learn about love, according to 1 Corinthians 13:4-8a.** Read it aloud. Ask: **When you played tennis, when did you feel patient? kind? not jeal-**

89

ous? happy? When was it difficult to feel those feelings? How did you feel when I called your serve "out" when you knew it was "in"? How do you show the "love" ingredients in your everyday life?

Ask kids each to put their racket in front of them on the grass. Say: **Your racket strings represent a "love ingredient graph" to help you rank each love ingredient in your life. The center of your racket represents perfection in love. The farther away from the center you go, the less you show a particular love ingredient in your life. I'll say one love ingredient from the passage. Think about it, then poke your finger through your** racket in the place you'd rank that ingredient in your life.

After naming each ingredient below, have kids show their rankings to a person sitting close to them. Here are the ingredients: patient, kind, not jealous, doesn't brag, not proud, not rude, not selfish, not upset with others, doesn't count up wrongs, is happy with the truth, accepts all things, trusts, hopes, and is strong.

As kids get ready to leave, have them say which ingredient they most want to work on. Close with a prayer: **God, help us truly love each other in the way you intended—especially when we don't feel like it. In Jesus' name, amen.**

44

Video Arcade

Theme: Distractions

Scripture to Go: Hebrews 2:1-4

So we must be more careful to follow what we were taught. Then we will not stray away from the truth. The teaching God spoke through angels was shown to be true, and anyone who did not follow it or obey it received the punishment that was earned. So surely we also will be punished if we ignore this great salvation. The Lord himself first told about this salvation, and it was proven true to us by those who heard him. God also proved it by using wonders, great signs, many kinds of miracles, and by giving people gifts through the Holy Spirit, just as he wanted.

Devotion to Go

As kids play at the arcade, choose two volunteers to go around the room and act as "disrupters"—people who try to distract group members from the games they're playing. After everyone has been disrupted, gather around any video game that displays a character trying to reach a goal while avoiding many objects along the way.

Ask: **Have you had fun so far? How many of you felt distracted at some point as you played a game? Who distracted you? How did it feel to be distracted? How is being distracted in your video game like being distracted from following God?**

91

Say: **All kinds of things in our daily lives can distract us from following God. Just like the video-game characters try to make it through mazes, we too have to make our way through a maze of life's distractions. God wants us to be focused on him—not distracted away from his love and direction.**

Ask for a volunteer to try his or her luck with the video game you're standing by. Have the other kids gather around and try to help the player win the game. (If you have more than seven people, form groups of four and have someone in each group play a game.) Then read aloud Hebrews 2:1-4.

Ask: **How is concentrating on the game like not "straying from the truth"? How is helping each other on the games like helping each other follow Jesus? How can we do that in real life? What things in your life distract you from following Jesus?**

Go around the group and have kids each say one way they can try and lessen the distractions that keep them from Jesus. Pray: **God, help us resist life's distractions and carefully follow what we've been taught. Use your power to help us follow you and be the best we can be. In Jesus' name, amen.**

45 Volleyball

Theme:
Time management

Scripture to Go: Ecclesiastes 8:5b
A wise person does the right thing at the right time.

Devotion to Go

Gather at a gymnasium or community center and play volleyball. Try lots of variations, such as using two volleyballs instead of one, or using a balloon, beach ball, Nerf ball or small bean bag for a ball. Lastly, throw lots of balls into the game and have kids try to keep all of them in the air.

Take a break from volleyball. Ask: **How did you feel playing volleyball in so many different ways? How was that like dealing with the sudden changes that happen in our daily schedules? How did you feel playing volleyball with all the balls at the end? How was that like juggling lots of activities in life? What is difficult about it? What activities do you try to juggle in your lives?** Ask the last person who served to read aloud Ecclesiastes 8:5b. Ask: **How does this passage apply to what we just experienced? How might this passage apply to our lives?**

Spread out in a large circle. Serve the ball to a person, and ask him or her to say one activity that takes time in his or her life. Then have that person serve the ball to someone else and say one activity that takes time in his or her life. Repeat the process until each person has had a chance to respond. Ask: **How can we manage our time better? How can we set priorities, so we don't do everything for everybody?**

Repeat the previous activity, only this time when a person catches the ball, have him or her say one time-management idea, such as "learn to say no." Do this until each person has a chance to respond.

Join hands and pray: **God, we can't be all things to all people. Help us know when to say no and when to say yes. Help us prioritize our calendars, putting you first. In Jesus' name, amen.**

46 Walkathon

Theme: God's guidance

Scripture to Go: Isaiah 30:19-21
You people who live on Mount Zion in Jerusalem will not cry any-more. The Lord will hear your crying, and he will comfort you. When he hears you, he will help you. The Lord has given you sorrow and hurt like the bread and water you ate every day. He is your teacher; he will not continue to hide from you, but you will see your teacher with your own eyes. If you go the wrong way—to the right or to the left—you will hear a voice behind you saying, "This is the right way. You should go this way."

Devotion to Go

Before you begin your walkathon, gather for a send-off devotion. Give kids each a map of the route. Ask: **How do you feel about going on this walk? Have you ever walked this route before? How will you know which way to go? How is God's guidance like this map?**

Have a volunteer read aloud Isaiah 30:19-21. Ask: **What does this passage say about God's help in choosing the right paths in life? How is paying attention to God's directions the same as following the course markings in today's walkathon? How is it differ-ent? What happens if you go off-course in the walkathon? What happens in real life if you wander off from the way**

God wants you to go? How can we listen to God's directions in our life? How does he speak to us today?

Have kids each think of a problem they need God's help and guidance with. Have them keep it in mind as you say the following send-off paraphrase: **You people who go to church at** (*fill in the name of your church*) **in** (*fill in the name of your city*) **will not cry anymore.**

He will hear your crying as you name problems you need help with (*have kids quietly name problems*), and he will comfort you. When he hears you he will help you. When you go on your walk today, God is with you. When you walk through life, pray to God and listen to him. He will tell you, "This is the right way. You should go this way."

47 Water Skiing

Theme: God's power

Scripture to Go: Ephesians 1:19-23
And you will know that God's power is very great for us who believe. That power is the same as the great strength God used to raise Christ from the dead and put him at his right side in the heavenly world. God has put Christ over all rulers, authorities, powers, and kings, not only in this world but also in the next. God put everything under his power and made him the head over everything for the church, which is Christ's body. The church is filled with Christ, and Christ fills everything in every way.

Devotion to Go

Give everyone an opportunity to water ski. Those who don't want to water ski can take turns riding in the boat and watching. During the day, have volunteers attempt to water ski with the boat going as slow as possible. Take a break, and gather on the shore for a devotion.

Ask: **Where does the boat get its power? How does it feel when the boat is pulling you around the lake? How does it feel when you let go of the rope? When water skiing, why is it important for the boat to have enough power? How did it feel to water ski with the boat going slow? How is that like the way you feel when you don't sense God's power?**

Have a person who has water skied for the first time read aloud Ephesians 1:19-23. Ask: **How is water skiing behind a powerful boat like God's power in our lives? When has God's power pulled you out of a "sinking" situation? How does God's power make it possible for us to enjoy life? What activities make us let go of our power source—like the choppy waves sometimes made us let go of the rope? What are some sources of "false power" young people** turn to today? Say: **The passage tells us God's power is great for us who believe. Let's go around and finish this thought, "God's power is so great, I can . . . "**

After you finish the sentence, go around the group and have everyone else complete the thought. Pray: **Dear God, help us resist the temptation to be "dragged down" by rough situations. Help us remember that you're our power source for life every day. In Jesus' name, amen.**

48 Youth Rally

**Theme:
Making friends**

Scripture to Go: John 15:12-17
"This is my command: Love each other as I have loved you. The greatest love a person can show is to die for his friends. You are my friends if you do what I command you. I no longer call you servants, because a servant does not know what his master is doing. But I call you friends, because I have made known to you everything I heard from my Father. You did not choose me; I chose you. And I gave you this work: to go and produce fruit, fruit that will last. Then the Father will give you anything you ask for in my name. This is my command: Love each other."

Devotion to Go

If your regional youth rally lasts several days, gather as a youth group each night. Have a worship service with prayers, singing and thoughts of the day's events. On the first night, gather with your group members and count the number of people in your group. On the second night, ask group members to each bring one friend. Have kids join you in counting the number of people. On the third night (if your gathering goes on for more nights), ask kids each to invite two friends. Once again, count the number of kids.

Toward the end of the gathering, use this devotion. Ask kids each to bring their program (which lists the schedule for the gathering events).

Read aloud John 15:12-17. Ask: **How did you feel inviting new friends each night of our devotions? How is that like the way God made us his friends, like it says in this passage? How do you feel knowing that making friends makes you more like Jesus? What does it mean to be a friend, according to this passage? How can we be friends with Jesus?**

Ask the visitors: **How did you feel being asked to come to our youth group meeting? How is that like the way God includes us in his life?**

Say: **We've made lots of friends during this event, but let's remember the greatest friend of all—Jesus. Always make him the central relationship in your life.** Pray: **Dear God, it's fun to gather with so many friends for worship. As we return home, help us continue our friendships there—especially our friendship with you. In Jesus' name, amen.**

Have a program-signing party. Let group members and their new friends sign each other's programs with "You're a wonderful person because..." affirmations. Be sure to exchange names and addresses so kids can stay in touch.

49 Zoo

Theme: Creation caretakers

Scripture to Go: Genesis 7:1-5
Then the Lord said to Noah, "I have seen that you are the best person among the people of this time, so you and your family can go into the boat. Take with you seven pairs, each male with its female, of every kind of clean animal, and take one pair, each male with its female, of every kind of unclean animal. Take seven pairs of all the birds of the sky, each male with its female. This will allow all these animals to continue living on the earth after the flood. Seven days from now I will send rain on the earth. It will rain forty days and forty nights, and I will wipe off from the earth every living thing that I have made."
  Noah did everything the Lord commanded him.

Devotion to Go

Get with zoo officials and plan a time when your group can go and care for the animals, such as feed seals, feed baby monkeys or clean cages. Afterward, tour the zoo. Have kids notice the signs of animals who are in danger of extinction.

Gather for the devotion. Ask: **How did it feel to care for the zoo animals? How is that similar to the way God wants us to care for his creation? How is it different?**

Ask kids how many pets they have at home. Have the one with the most pets read aloud Genesis 7:1-5. Have kids each tell which zoo animal they liked best. Then ask kids to imagine a world without that animal. Ask: **Why did God save Noah and his family? What qualities do you think Noah portrayed in his life? Why would God want to save all the animals? Which animals today are in need of saving? What do we do today that may harm animals?** Say: **God warned Noah that he would send the rain in seven days, so he had a week to round up the animals and make them safe.**

Ask: **What are warnings we've seen today that tell us animals are in danger? How can we listen to these warnings and respond before it's too late?**

Have kids brainstorm ways they can help care for God's creation. Ask everyone to choose one suggestion and begin to do it this week. Pray: **Dear God, how wonderful your world is! Help us each to commit ourselves to better care of your creation and all creatures great and small. In Jesus' name, amen.**

50

On the way to an activity

Theme: Anticipation and anxiety

Scripture to Go: Philippians 4:6-7
Do not worry about anything, but pray and ask God for everything you need, always giving thanks. And God's peace, which is so great we cannot understand it, will keep your hearts and minds in Christ Jesus.

Devotion to Go

Photocopy this devotion for each car or van load of kids. Do the devotion on the way to your activity.

Have the person who's sitting next to the driver read aloud Philippians 4:6-7. Ask: **When you look forward to this event, what do you anticipate? What do you think the activity will be like? What excites you? worries you? What's one thing you want to get out of the event? How is that like the** way you look forward to the future? What do you think your future will bring? What excites you? worries you? What one goal do you want to achieve for your future?

Pray the following prayer, pausing so kids can silently fill in the blanks: **God, you tell us to not worry about anything, but to pray about everything. Hear us as we pray for ourselves, our safety and this upcoming event (*pause*). Hear us as we pray for our futures, about our worries and anxi-**

eties, and our goals (*pause*). You tell us to always give thanks. Hear the things we are thankful for (*pause*).

Please fill us with your peace, right now, during our upcoming event and the rest of our lives. In Jesus' name, amen.

51

When the van breaks down

Theme: Worry

Scripture to Go: 1 Peter 5:7
Give all your worries to him, because he cares about you.

Devotion to Go

Gather the kids in a circle in a shady area, or protected area away from the broken-down vehicle.

Ask: **How do you feel about the van breaking down? What worries you most about it? How is that like the way we feel when bad things happen in life? How should we deal with our worries?**

Have the person who looks least worried read aloud 1 Peter 5:7. Ask: **What does the passage tell us to do with all our worries?**

Place a Bible in the center of the circle. Say: **We're going to have a chance to give all our worries to God, because he cares for us.**

Have kids each cup their hands, like they're holding a worry. Go around the circle and let kids each explain their worry, such as getting the vehicle fixed, getting home safely or worrying their parents. After explaining their worry, have them each place their worry on the Bible to symbolize giving it to God. Say: **God hears all our worries—today and every day of our lives. He takes care of us.**

Let's go around one more time. This time say one thing you're thankful for. Close by praying: Thank you, God, for being such a good listener with our worries. Help us have faith in you even when we can't see the immediate answer to our prayers. In Jesus' name, amen.

52 When bad weather cancels an event

Theme: Disappointment

Scripture to Go: 1 John 5:3-5 and John 16:33

Loving God means obeying his commands. And God's commands are not too hard for us, because everyone who is a child of God conquers the world. And this is the victory that conquers the world—our faith. So the one who wins against the world is the person who believes that Jesus is the Son of God.

I told you these things so that you can have peace in me. In this world you will have trouble, but be brave! I have defeated the world.

Devotion to Go

Gather the kids in the church by a window so you can see and hear the rain or storm. Ask: **How do you feel about the storm? How does it feel knowing we won't go to the event? What were you most looking forward to today? How are your feelings today like the disappointment we feel lots of times in life? Why is it difficult to change your plans when the unexpected happens? What other things happen in your daily life that cause disappointment?**

Have two volunteers read aloud 1 John 5:3-5 and John 16:33. Ask: **How do the two passages make you feel? How does it ease your sadness to know God has overcome the world and all the disappointing, unexpected things that**

happen? How can we deal positively with this situation and turn it to good?

List options to do instead of the event. You could:

● reschedule the event for another date and time;

● take a walk in the storm right now;

● (if it's raining or snowing) go outside, open your mouths and catch the raindrops or snowflakes;

● play board games and sing songs; or

● make or order pizza.

Pray: **Dear God, help us learn to take the good with the bad. When disappointments threaten to bring us down, help us look on the bright side so we can know your peace. In Jesus' name, amen.**

Choose one of your brainstorm ideas and do it!